Wakefield Libraries
& Information Services

D0531468

50s
OD
JRES

This book should be returned by the last date stamped above. You may renew the loan personally, by post or telephone for a further period if the book is not required by another reader.

A 1950s
CHILDHOOD
IN PICTURES

PAUL FEENEY

The
History
Press

All images in this book © Mary Evans Picture Library with individual
contributors listed by each image where applicable

Individual contributors for cover images: front: Roger Mayne; *back left:* Roger
Mayne; *back centre:* John Gay/English Heritage; *back right:* Henry Grant

First published 2014

The History Press
The Mill, Brimscombe Port
Stroud, Gloucestershire, GL5 2QG
www.thehistorypress.co.uk

© Paul Feeney, 2014

British Library Cataloguing in Publication Data.
A catalogue record for this book is available from the British Library.

ISBN 978 0 7509 5295 8

Production managed by Jellyfish
Printed in Malta by Melita Press

CONTENTS

Introduction   7

1   The Streets & Bomb Sites   11
2   School Life   39
3   Out & About   69
4   Home Life   89
5   High Days, Holidays & Events   107

     Index   127

INTRODUCTION

I was born in London in 1948 and was fortunate enough to have grown up at a time when it was still possible for children to play out in the streets without fear of traffic and with little hindrance from parked cars. The backstreets were our playgrounds, and the bomb sites and derelict houses left in the wake of the Second World War were where we played out our adventures and rummaged for buried treasures. Life in Britain was so very different then; the nation was still recovering from the ravages of war, the country was bankrupt and times were very hard for ordinary working families. However, because of the wartime bravery of our parents and grandparents in successfully defeating Nazism, our generation had the good fortune to grow up in a peaceful country in which we were free to enjoy a happy and untroubled childhood.

This was a time of severe austerity; wartime rationing continued until well after the war ended. Sweet and sugar rationing continued until 1953, and it wasn't until July 1954 that we saw the end of rationing altogether. But, after government-imposed rationing formally ended, some things were still difficult to get hold of, even if you could afford to buy them. For ordinary working families, times were hard throughout the fifties and many didn't begin to see improvements in their lifestyles until well into the 1960s. The ravages of war were still etched in the faces of our parents and it was clear that their memories of wartime destruction and misery would never die. We lived in damp and draughty houses with no hot water and outside lavatories, and in winter, the outside air was often polluted with dense killer smog. Our day-to-day lives were very simple: we enjoyed none of the technological wizardry of today; we didn't even have a television or a telephone in our homes. No fridge, freezer, washing machine, microwave, central heating, stereo; we had none of these things. In 1950, there were less than 2 million cars on the road in Britain and few of these were owned by ordinary working families. We didn't even have the right sort of clothes and shoes to keep us warm and dry in bad weather. Yes, these were austere times and it is easy to paint a completely dark and gloomy picture of the 1950s; the history books generally portray it as a bleak period wedged between the war-torn 1940s and the 'swinging sixties', but this is not the uppermost image in my mind when I look back on my 1950s childhood. You see, as children we didn't know any other way of life; we had been born into these times of hardship and we knew no different. Up until 1954, we thought the rationing of food and goods was a normal way of life and that it had always been that way. We just got on with our childhood and made the best of it, and from what I can remember, we children had a lot of fun.

I hope the pictures in this book will give you a good insight into what a 1950s childhood in Britain was really like, especially in the capital city of London, and I hope it will help to dispel the myth that some like to promote of miserable, snotty-nosed urchins littering the streets. There was a baby boom in the early post-war years and it is clear that there was an abundance of children around during the 1950s, but the image in my mind is of happy, fun-loving children with lots of smiling faces and loads of laughter. When we weren't at school, we spent as much time as possible playing outside, and we were never short of playmates. We had few shop-bought toys and so we made our own out of discarded bits of wood and metal we found around the bomb sites. We made our own bows and arrows, and carved toy guns and rifles out of lumps of wood to play cowboys and Indians, and we used old pram wheels, planks of wood and orange boxes to make our own go-karts. We were very industrious; it came naturally to us to make use of any old discarded stuff we found when we were out on our adventures. We had endless hours of fun playing with very basic things, whether it was a length of rope, a piece of chalk, a lump of wood or a tennis ball. We also made use of every piece of street furniture – from lampposts to street signs – for climbing and swinging from. We explored every inch of any derelict houses we came across and climbed every tree there was to climb. As the pictures in this book will testify, we had fun!

It is hard to compare childhood in Britain today with how it was back in the 1950s. No doubt childhood today is equally fun-packed, just different. I feel privileged to have experienced the joys of a 1950s childhood. There was something very special about it: a carefree childhood in what was to be the last decade in which children were able to retain their childish innocence well into their secondary school years and enjoy an untroubled young life, full of fun and games. There were no pressures on us to grow up too soon; the stresses of adolescence and then adult life could wait. We were lucky.

Finally, I would like to pay tribute and thank all of the talented photographers who created the wonderful pictures that appear in this book. These images capture the mood of the 1950s childhood I remember and I am so pleased that these photographers had the skill and foresight to record these images for children of the 1950s to look back on, and also enable later generations to see and enjoy the atmosphere of these bygone times. I hope my accompanying captions will adequately explain the action in each picture and that you will enjoy the experience of looking back on a 1950s childhood.

Paul Feeney

The Streets & Bomb Sites

An express dairy milkman is being harassed by a group of children who are playing around his milk float as he tries to make his deliveries to these post-war, temporary prefabricated houses in Battersea, south-west London. (*c.* 1957) *(Roger Mayne)*

Opposite: A little girl struggles to stay within the lines as she plays hopscotch on the Harrow Road, London. Hopscotch was one of a number of favourite street games played by children in the 1950s. (*c.* 1958) *(Roger Mayne)*

Everyone, in every age group, enjoyed playing card games. We played cards together in family groups, and children even occupied themselves by playing solo games alone on rainy days. As in this picture, groups of children were often seen playing various types of card games on front doorsteps. These boys are playing on the front steps of a house in North Kensington, London. (*c.* 1959) (*Roger Mayne*)

Children playing with their home-made go-kart. The boy on the go-kart is steering it with his feet with the aid of a length of rope; the other small boy pushes while a little girl runs behind. Children regularly made these for themselves using old wooden crates, bits of wood and the wheels from discarded prams. (1950s) *(Roger Mayne)*

A group of Glasgow children play in the street, riding their bicycles and clambering on a parked tanker. Large vehicles such as this were just too tempting for children to resist climbing on. (*c.* 1958) *(Roger Mayne)*

Two small girls doing handstands against a corrugated fence in a street in west London, with no fear and not a thought for who might see their baggy knickers. Girls regularly practised handstands and cartwheels in the street. These skills were not usually taught at primary school; young girls just copied the acrobatics they saw older girls doing. (*c.* 1956) *(Roger Mayne)*

Opposite: Autumn 1957 in North Kensington, London, where two boys prepare for battle by threading string through their respective conkers as they ready themselves for a traditional game of conkers, and probably some bruised knuckles in the process. (1957) *(Roger Mayne)*

Four girls of different ages are skipping together in the middle of the street, while two small boys watch them from a distance. It always intrigued boys as to how girls could skip for ages without getting tangled up in the rope. (*c.* 1957) *(Roger Mayne)*

Children and teenagers playing cricket in the street at Brindley Road, Paddington, in London. With so little traffic around at the time, it's unlikely they will need to move out of the road to let a vehicle pass. (*c.* 1957) *(Roger Mayne)*

Boys and girls at the empty windows of a bombed building in Bermondsey, south-east London. There were countless numbers of bombed and derelict buildings around London in the 1950s; these were the unofficial playgrounds of 1950s children. (*c*. 1956) (*Roger Mayne*)

Four young girls perform a dance in the middle of Southam Street, west London. Some girls were taught to dance at school while others mimicked what they saw the others doing. (*c.* 1956) (*Roger Mayne*)

Three little girls drawing chalk figures on the road in North Kensington, London. The funny thing is that nobody ever seemed to buy any chalk but someone always had a stick tucked away in a deep recess of one of their pockets. (*c.* 1956) *(Roger Mayne)*

Girls loved to dress up in their mothers' clothes and slap on lipstick and face powder; then they would parade up and down the street in high-heeled shoes, proud as punch. These two young London girls look almost ready to parade. (*c.* 1958) *(Roger Mayne)*

Boys were often asked by girls to secure ropes around the top of lampposts so that they could swing around on them. The children standing on the back bumper of a vehicle on Clarendon Crescent in west London appear to be waiting for the boys to finish tying the rope so that they can have a go. (*c.* 1959) *(Roger Mayne)*

Opposite: Two little girls playing on a west London street together. One of them is pulling the other along on roller skates. In the 1950s, roller skates were quite primitive and it was often hard to get the wheels to turn; sometimes you needed a pull or a push to get you going. A passing teenager watches the action. (*c.* 1956) *(Roger Mayne)*

Regardless of the danger, a couple of young kids are seen here larking about underneath a parked lorry while two others watch their antics. Lorry drivers would often check around their vehicles for mischievous kids and tell them to 'clear off' before driving away. (*c.* 1957) *(Roger Mayne)*

Opposite: This group of girls are having great fun rolling around in the road, roaring with laughter and not a care in the world. (*c.* 1956) *(Roger Mayne)*

A gang of boys are playing with an abandoned car next to a bomb site in west London. In the 1950s, policemen regularly walked the beat in all parts of London and young boys such as these would be on the lookout for their local bobby so that they could scarper when he came into view. (*c.* 1958) (*Roger Mayne*)

Two kids are fighting on the ground while the other children look on, in the Harrow Road area of London. A woman with a child have just gone by and probably taken no notice of what the kids are up to. This was all part of 'playing out'. (*c.* 1957) (*Roger Mayne*)

A little boy with a bandaged knee covers his face on a bomb site (twelve years after the end of the Second World War) in Waverley Walk, west London. The two boys in the background carry on rummaging regardless. (*c.* 1957) (*Roger Mayne*)

Four mischievous girls larking about while hanging from a lamppost in St Stephen's Gardens, London. I doubt there is a child of the 1950s who didn't climb a lamppost at some time in their childhood. (*c.* 1957) (*Roger Mayne*)

A street scene like this could be seen anywhere in Britain in the 1950s and early 1960s. In this picture, three young girls are skipping in the middle of a deserted Manchester road. (*c.* 1959) (*Shirley Baker*)

A comical kerbside picture of two young boys and their pet dog exploring the contents of a drain after having removed the cover. (*c.* 1959) (*Shirley Baker*)

Three boys half kneeling on the pavement in Hampden Crescent, west London, playing a game of marbles. (*c.* 1957) *(Roger Mayne)*

Children play in the ruins of a house on a bomb site in Bermondsey, south-east London. Children would stage many of their adventures in the bombed-out ruins of buildings like this one, from cops and robbers to pirates, and hide and seek was always a favourite. It was dangerous but fun. (*c.* 1954) (*Roger Mayne*)

Opposite: Three boys play at cowboys in Hampden Crescent, west London. One of them wears a large hat and is riding on the back of another boy. The third boy wears a scarf round his face, like a bandit. Graffiti was not a problem in the 1950s. What little of it there was would usually be in chalk and it would be drawn on the side of derelict buildings and on bomb sites. (*c.* 1957) (*Roger Mayne*)

These children are thoroughly enjoying themselves as they dance in a ring in the roadway in St Stephen's Gardens, west London. There was always an abundance of children with smiling faces playing in the streets. (*c.* 1957) (*Roger Mayne*)

A group of seven children – five girls and two boys – hang out on the pavement in North Kensington, London. On the brick wall behind them someone has chalked 'WIPE SUEZ OUT' (this picture was taken shortly after the Suez Crisis). (*c.* 1957) (*Roger Mayne*)

A group of mischievous boys play bows and arrows outside and inside what looks like a rather old black taxi cab in the North Kensington area of London. These boys would have made these toys themselves, and note there are no rubber stoppers on the ends of the arrows they are about to fire. (*c.* 1957) *(Roger Mayne)*

Two girls playing on a street corner in west London. The smaller girl swings from a rope attached to a lamppost. Other children are approaching on scooters and a young man attempts to pass between them unscathed. (*c.* 1957) *(Roger Mayne)*

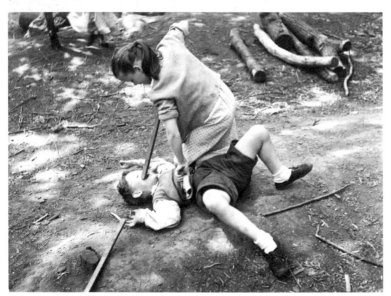

A girl and a boy are playing together on a patch of waste ground in the Holland Park area of London. They are using long sticks as swords and, having got the better of the boy, the girl looks as if she is about to finish him off. (*c.* 1956) *(Roger Mayne)*

These four boys are pictured in Hampden Crescent, off Harrow Road, Paddington, west London. One is climbing a drainpipe up to a first-floor window, while another two are loading pieces of wood on to a home-made cart. You would see a lot of this kind of wood-collecting activity in the days leading up to Bonfire Night each year. (c. 1957) *(Roger Mayne)*

A group of children are watching boys taking their turn to jump from Hilgay Bridge into the River Wissey in Norfolk. Isn't that what waterway bridges are for? Great fun on a warm summer's day. (c. 1956) *(John Gay/ English Heritage)*

What few motor cars there were in the 1950s were often unreliable and they sometimes needed a bit of help to get going. A group of boys are giving this car a push start in Princedale Road, west London. (*c.* 1957) (*Roger Mayne*)

Children play cricket on the cobbles in Addison Place, London, while others climb walls and drainpipes to get to a vantage viewpoint. (*c.* 1956) (*Roger Mayne*)

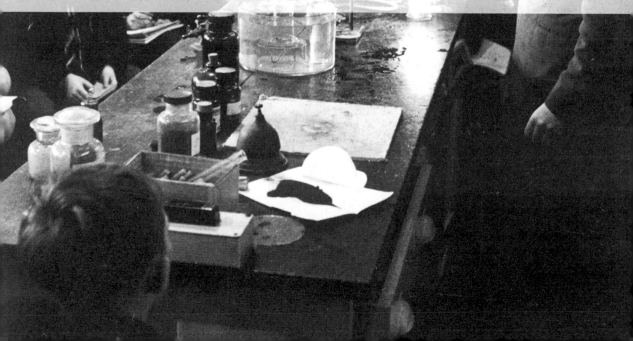

School Life

We all suffered indignity at the hands of the 'nit nurse' when she did her regular school visits to inspect our heads for small nasty creatures. In this picture, the nurse is having a good search of this boy's hair for any signs of head lice, and this was always done in front of the class. (*c. 1958*) *(Henry Grant)*

A classroom of teenage boys and girls sitting at their desks studying at Nevill County Secondary School in East Sussex. This would have been a typical classroom scene at the time. (*c. 1959*) *(Henry Grant)*

A troop of girls in school uniform walk in pairs across West Heath Road to Whitestone Pond on Hampstead Heath in London, under the watchful eye of a policeman. (*c. 1959*) *(John Gay/English Heritage)*

A fitness class in progress at Sarson School for Girls, Melton Mowbray in Leicestershire. This photograph shows a typical secondary school gymnasium used for physical education or PE lessons, as they were called. These schoolgirls are using various pieces of gym equipment, including hoops, wall bars and vaulting horses. (*c.* 1956) *(Henry Grant)*

These young children are enjoying the luxury of doing their PE lessons on a purpose-built climbing frame with ropes in their modern-for-the-time school gym at Danesfield County Primary School in Buckinghamshire. (*c.* 1959) *(Henry Grant)*

These young primary school children follow the story from their books as the teacher reads to the class at Hallfield School in Paddington. Note the very fashionable polka dot skirt worn by the teacher and the equally fashionable cardigan worn by the girl who is standing. (*c.* 1956) *(Roger Mayne)*

Opposite: Primary school children learning to play the recorder at Bramfield Primary School in Suffolk. Note the classroom walls are adorned with the usual school artwork and the typical school clock. (*c.* 1957) *(Henry Grant)*

During a school sports day, a very determined-looking boy carrying a baton sprints along the track watched by a group of schoolboys, some in shorts, others in their school uniform. (1950s) *(Gerald Wilson)*

Opposite: Boys and girls of various ages enjoy racing against one another in an organised sack race. This was one of several fun races; others included the egg-and-spoon race and the wheelbarrow race. (1950s) *(Gerald Wilson)*

A school netball game with one team wearing cloth sashes to identify team members. The girl on the right must be feeling the cold as she is still wearing her jumper. (1950s) *(Henry Grant)*

A group of young schoolgirls play the board game Ludo in a classroom. This might happen at lunchtime on a very wet day, when some schools would allow pupils to come in from the playground to the school buildings. (1950s) *(Henry Grant)*

Pupils tuck into their school dinners at the Dorothy Stringer Secondary School in Brighton, East Sussex. It looks a bit high-class compared to the average secondary school dining hall. Gravy boats and serving dishes were not the norm on school dinner tables. (*c.* 1956) *(Henry Grant)*

A class of children at Bramfield Primary School in Suffolk. It looks like this classroom is heated by a solid-fuel burning stove, which is shielded by a tall fireguard. (*c.* 1957) *(Henry Grant)*

A teacher supervises a group of primary school children playing a game of rounders in a local park. (*c.* 1959)

A class of primary school boys pulling various uninterested faces at St John's School in Kilburn, London. (*c.* 1959) *(Roger Mayne)*

A primary school dining hall with dinner ladies dishing up school dinners to a queue of hungry young children at Hallfield School in Paddington, London. (*c.* 1956) *(Roger Mayne)*

Opposite: These children are having a painting lesson at a London primary school. They are using huge brushes and large pots of watercolour paints. Note the girls' hairstyles and their dresses. (*c.* 1950) *(Sarah Lasenby)*

The teacher assists these children with their drawings and watercolour paintings while one little girl is peeping through the glass in the door. Their previous works of art are proudly displayed on the wall. (*c.* 1950) *(Sarah Lasenby)*

A class of teenage schoolgirls put on their own show using puppets they have made in craft classes at St Albans County Grammar School. (*c.* 1950) *(Sarah Lasenby)*

A class of teenage schoolgirls having a clay-modelling lesson at Brixton Central Girls' School in south London. One of the girls is making a model of a young woman; another is making a polar bear. (*c.* 1950) (*Sarah Lasenby*)

An art class at Brixton Central Girls' School. A class of teenage schoolgirls are drawing and painting two live models who are dressed up as a medieval king and queen. (*c.* 1950) *(Sarah Lasenby)*

A young teacher supervises these happy and lively boys and girls as they chase each other around the room in their stockinged feet at Aboyne Lodge Primary School in St Albans, Hertfordshire. (*c.* 1951) *(Sarah Lasenby)*

These school children are on a nature trail at Ranmore in Surrey. They are making notes as their teacher shows them infrared enlargements to indicate the characteristics of the landscape around them. (*c.* 1959)

Many schools had chess clubs and sometimes members would take part in tournaments between local schools. This young boy is studying the board before deciding which piece he should move next in this chess competition at Haselrigge School in Clapham, London. (1950s) *(Roger Mayne)*

Boys playing cricket in the playground at Hallfield Junior School in Paddington, west London. This was a new and very modern school at the time and its main building was later made a Grade 2* listed building. (Late 1950s) *(Roger Mayne)*

The police had a very visible presence on the streets in the 1950s. Police constables had their own regular beat to walk, but in addition to this they did traffic and road-crossing duty. In this picture, the policeman is helping a group of primary school children cross the road outside their school. (Early 1950s) *(Metropolitan Police Authority)*

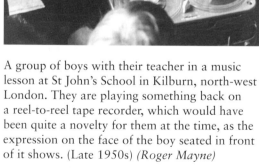

A group of boys with their teacher in a music lesson at St John's School in Kilburn, north-west London. They are playing something back on a reel-to-reel tape recorder, which would have been quite a novelty for them at the time, as the expression on the face of the boy seated in front of it shows. (Late 1950s) *(Roger Mayne)*

Children playing recorders during the Dartington Hall School Christmas festival. The school, near Totnes in Devon, which was founded in 1926 and closed in 1987, offered a progressive coeducational boarding life for its pupils. Unusually, it had no corporal punishment; in fact, it had no punishment at all. (*c.* 1959) *(Roger Mayne)*

Children in costume take part in a Nativity play during a Christmas festival at Dartington Hall School. (*c.* 1959) *(Roger Mayne)*

A teacher performs an experiment in front of a science class at Henry Thornton Grammar School in Clapham, south London. Note, as with all grammar schools, the school uniform was strictly adhered to. (*c.* 1959) (*Henry Grant*)

At a secondary school in Stoke-on-Trent, two boys are boxing in front of their classmates as part of their physical education. School children were encouraged to take part in as many sporting activities as possible; some sports were compulsory while others were voluntary. Boxing could be a bit scary for a 12-year-old secondary school boy because they were usually matched by weight rather than by age. (*c.* 1956) *(Henry Grant)*

Opposite: Some loved it and others loathed it, but like it or not, all children were given a free bottle of milk to drink at school each day. They came in special one-third of a pint bottles and you were strongly encouraged to drink it down – warm milk in summer and freezing cold milk in winter. (*c.* 1955) *(Henry Grant)*

Clockwise from left: These four schoolgirls are playing netball in their school hall. One girl takes a shot and the others await the rebound. Netball was a popular sport for girls and it was played competitively at secondary schools. Note the doors in the background; these were a typical design feature in most school buildings. (*c.* 1956); A boy performs an acrobatic jump and tumbles across four other boys, who are crouched on a gym mat on the floor. As his classmates watch and wait their turn, one boy on the left seems especially impressed with the performance. (*c.* 1956); A group of barefooted teenage schoolgirls holding tambourines are learning to be graceful and ladylike during a lesson of musical movement, involving stretching and dancing. Note the apparel of the students and their teacher. (*c.* 1956) *(All Henry Grant)*

This was in the days when schools remained open in bad weather and children trudged to school in all sorts of inclement conditions. These primary school children are playing happily in the snow-covered playground of St Mary's School in Hertfordshire, and note all the boys are in short trousers. Schools were often linked with churches and they worked together to provide children with an all-round Christian, academic and sports education. The tower of St Mary's church can be seen behind the school buildings. (1950s) *(John Gay/English Heritage)*

These Metropolitan Police officers are teaching road safety to a large group of very young children. The man in the white outfit with traffic lights on his front is Safety Sam, a character invented to encourage children to think about road safety. A sergeant stands with four little girls in the foreground, and a large audience of children watches from the other side of the road. (*c. 1950*) *(Metropolitan Police Authority)*

A large group of schoolgirls in brightly braided school blazers are gathered to watch a game of lacrosse. Four members of the team stand at the front, not too eager to remove their blazers; they do look cold! (*c. 1959*) *(Roger Mayne)*

Out & About

These three young boys are trying to decide what to buy from this open-fronted newsagents and confectioners in Latimer Road, west London. With their limited funds, will it be comics or sweets? (*c.* 1957) *(Roger Mayne)*

For many children, the highlight of their week was going to Saturday Morning Pictures at the local cinema. With children-only audiences, they could see all of their favourite film clips and characters, from *The Lone Ranger* to *Zorro*, Mr Pastry to Shirley Temple, and Charlie Chaplin to Buster Keaton, not forgetting the featured Westerns, during which they would boo the baddies and cheer the goodies. In this picture, one young boy is so overcome by the action that he can't bring himself to watch. (*c.* 1959) (*Maurice Ambler Collection*)

Some areas were lucky enough to have a local youth club where older children and teenagers could gather and play games. Table tennis was popular but many were happy to spend the evening playing board and card games. Chess, dominoes and cribbage were very popular games, as can be seen in this picture, which was taken at the King's Youth Hostel in Dolgellau, Wales. (1950s)

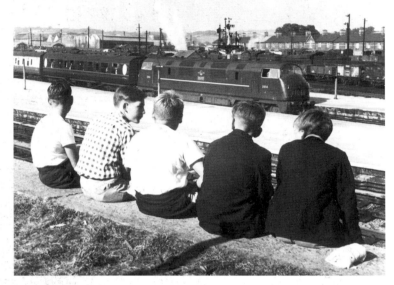

These five boys are enjoying a day's trainspotting at Newton Abbot station in Devon. At the platform is the 'Royal Duchy', with British Rail diesel engine *Dragon* at the head. (1950s)

These three boys are fishing for crabs from the pier of the Corporation Bridge across the River Freshney in Grimsby, Lincolnshire. (1950s)

Opposite: This kind of idyllic scene with four boys fishing on a riverbank could relate to any generation, but this picture was taken in the 1950s, and the Middle Mill (formerly called the King's Mill) in the background is now sadly demolished. The boys are fishing in the River Colne in Colchester. (1950s)

A crush on the steps as a group of children queue for their turn on the playground slide. A familiar scene as one of the girls suddenly realises it's far too high for her and she turns to go back down. (*c.* 1950) *(Margaret Monck)*

A young mother out shopping with her children and pram on a street in North Kensington, London. Note there are no parking restrictions. (Late 1950s) *(Roger Mayne)*

It looks like the two boys on the left are giving the smartly dressed boy a hard time, while other boys watch from the shop doorway of J.W. Bentley & Sons' tobacconists and confectioners in Biddulph, Staffordshire. It was not unusual for smartly dressed kids to get picked on, especially if they were wearing a brightly coloured or extra-smart school uniform. (*c.* 1955) *(Francis Frith)*

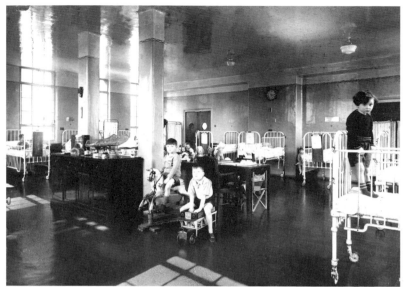

Children's Lady Iris Ward in the Princess Beatrice Hospital in London's Brompton Road. Note the children are wearing normal clothes rather than pyjamas, even the boy standing on his bed. This hospital closed in 1978. (*c.* 1950) *(Francis Frith)*

Children queuing for Saturday Morning Pictures at a cinema in the Harrow Road area of west London. Note the children are unsupervised and yet they are forming an orderly queue. Also notice the assortment of children's casual wear. (*c.* 1957) *(Roger Mayne)*

Shoppers and holidaymakers are looking at goods for sale in a shop window. The young boys are looking at things like buckets and spades for the beach, while a young girl sits on the pavement in the sunshine. (*c.* 1959) *(John Gay/English Heritage)*

Two boys are sat on their bikes on a small wooden bridge in the Hampshire countryside, looking down towards the stream below. It was quite normal for kids to wear the same clothes for school and for casual wear. The boy in front looks like he is wearing the sort of jacket, short trousers, pullover and shirt that he would wear for school. (Early 1950s) *(John Gay/English Heritage)*

Opposite: This young girl is enjoying a bike ride on her traditional 1950s bicycle, complete with front basket. The coat she is wearing is typical children's wear for the period. (*c.* 1955) *(John Gay/English Heritage)*

These children are playing on a newly built adventure playground in Pimlico, south-west London. As usual, the boys are climbing while the young girl is happy to stay closer to the ground. (*c.* 1958) *(Roger Mayne)*

Opposite: Although there were few cars around in the 1950s, young boys always managed to find an abandoned car to play with, whether in town or country. This boy is playing in the shell of an old car in a farmyard. (*c.* 1956) *(John Gay/English Heritage)*

A little boy stands outside an open-fronted Edinburgh shop. The shop window has displays of penknives, toy cars and other items. Outside on the pavement are headlines from the *Reveille* and *Daily Record*. (*c.* 1958) (*Roger Mayne*)

Three sisters walking hand in hand down a street of Victorian terraced houses. The two older girls are looking after their baby sister: a common occurrence and a normal part of family life. (Early 1950s) *(Heinz Zinram Collection)*

Metropolitan Police and London Fire Brigade attending a fire at Chelsea FC. This photograph by Sub-Inspector C.R.C. Turner shows Inspector A.J. Jones (Officer in Charge) and others at Walham Green, Fulham Road, London SW6, with a London Fire Brigade engine in the background. (*c.* 1956) *(Metropolitan Police Authority)*

A police officer using a police public call box on a London street. The Metropolitan Police introduced police boxes throughout the London area between 1928 and 1937. The one pictured is a Mackenzie Trench-style police box, made famous by the long-running television series *Doctor Who*. The boxes were installed so that members of the public could make emergency calls to the police, but many are now disused or have been withdrawn from service because of the prevalence of the mobile phone. (1950s) *(Metropolitan Police Authority)*

A horse-drawn rag-and-bone cart standing on the road opposite the United Dairies premises at 14 St Alban's Grove in Kensington, London, with part of the Builders Arms public house visible to the right of the frame. (*c.* 1959) *(John Gay/English Heritage)*

One of the last London trams crosses a quiet
Westminster Bridge, having just passed the Houses
of Parliament, which can be seen in the background.
On the side of the tram is a poster proclaiming 'Last
Tram Week'. The very last London tram ended its
final journey at south-east London's New Cross depot
in the early hours of the morning on 6 July 1952.
(*c.* 1952) *(Interfoto)*

This is an example of
traffic congestion on
Watford Way, Mill Hill,
in north London in the
1950s. A nice picture of
some lovely cars from
that period. (*c.* 1955)
Francis Frith)

After parking his barrow by the kerb, the
rag-and-bone man and another man kneel
over a pile of small pieces of scrap metal by
the roadside in a street of terraced houses in
Islington, north London. As always, there
is a pram parked outside one of the houses
nearby. (*c.* 1959) *(John Gay/English Heritage)*

View of the front window of a toyshop from
the inside looking out. It's Christmas and a
crowd of shoppers and children are watching
a table-top display of small mechanical toys.
(Late 1950s) *(John Gay/English Heritage)*

Nine Boy Scouts of the 1st Coulsdon Group sit around a table learning Morse code, under the watchful eye of their Scout Leader. (*c.* 1950) *(The Scout Association)*

A teacher giving lessons to child patients in a makeshift classroom at St Ann's Hospital in Tottenham, north London. The boy on the right has raised his hand to indicate he knows the answer to the question the teacher is asking. (*c.* 1955) *(Epic)*

Home Life

A young girl in Paddington, west London, leans across the handle of a pram to read her comic, totally ignoring the baby she is minding in the pram. (*c.* 1955) *(Roger Mayne)*

The simple pleasures of reading through the pages of *The Beano* and *The Dandy* comics were an essential part of a child's weekly entertainment. This boy's face says it all: do not disturb! (*c.* 1956) *(Roger Mayne)*

Few families had the good fortune to have their very own car, but those who did were proud of the fact and they were always willing to strike a pose to show off their pride and joy, as with this smartly dressed lady, her husband at the wheel of their Singer car and their son in the back. (*c.* 1950) (*Gill Stoker*)

Opposite: Most households burned coal in open fireplaces to heat their main living rooms. The chimney sweep was a regular visitor but for house-proud mums he was an unwelcome one: however careful he was with his filthy brushes and no matter how many sheets he used to protect the room from escaping soot, he usually left some dusty evidence of his visit on the furniture. (*c.* 1950)

Two women putting wet clothes through a floor-standing mangle to wring them out before hanging them on a washing line in the garden to dry. Wash days were a real chore because everything was done manually. When off school, the children of the house were often made to work the mangle for their mum. (1950s) *(Simon Roberts)*

A traditional British lounge interior, with comfy armchairs and brown wooden tables and chairs, heavily patterned wallpaper and the occasional rug or mat on a lino-covered floor. Although not in view here, there is bound to be a big, old valve radio somewhere in the room. (1950s)

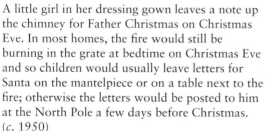

A little girl in her dressing gown leaves a note up the chimney for Father Christmas on Christmas Eve. In most homes, the fire would still be burning in the grate at bedtime on Christmas Eve and so children would usually leave letters for Santa on the mantelpiece or on a table next to the fire; otherwise the letters would be posted to him at the North Pole a few days before Christmas. (c. 1950)

A young stamp collector is seen here sticking stamps into his album. Stamp collecting was a very popular hobby for both boys and girls; it gave children a greater understanding of the geography of the world. It was an interest that could be shared between friends; they would swap stamps between themselves to make up sets or get rid of ones they already had. (1950s) *(Tony Boxall)*

These teenagers are playing cards in the open doorway of a house in west London. This pastime was not confined to teenagers: children of all ages regularly played cards and board games on doorsteps and in hallways, more so in fine weather. (*c.* 1957) *(Roger Mayne)*

A coalman carries in a large sack of coal for a terraced house in Salford, Manchester. He is being watched attentively by a young boy standing next to an elegant Victorian gas street lamp. (1950s) *(Shirley Baker)*

A television set was a rare sight in working-class homes until the late 1950s or early 1960s. This lucky family have one, though, and it looks a good size one for the era. The screen sizes of most television sets in the 1950s were between 9 and 14 inches, and up until 1955, when ITV began broadcasting, there was only one channel to watch: the BBC. (*c.* 1959) *(Interfoto)*

This young girl is playing with what looks like an open-fronted, home-made doll's house, and a nice collection of dolls. A doll's house was at the top of every young girl's list of Christmas presents, but because they were so expensive to buy, they were often home-made by dad. (1950s) *(H. Armstrong Roberts)*

A policeman walking his beat stops to exchange a few words with a lady sitting by the open window of a house in west London, while a neighbour watches and listens from a nearby doorway. Note the apron, which was the usual form of daywear for stay-at-home mums or housewives. Just out of sight there is a baby in the pram, who is enjoying a dose of fresh London air. (*c.* 1956) *(Roger Mayne)*

A village scene showing a man in a flat cap leaning over the gate of a cottage in Culmstock village, East Devon. This would have been an unusual sight in the 1950s: a man left to look after the baby! In mum's absence a baby would normally be left in the care of other siblings or a neighbour; dad would not have been top of the list for baby minding. (*c.* 1959) *(John Gay/English Heritage)*

Christmas time in the living room with one young boy in a cowboy hat observing two other children reading. The dog is hoping they are all too preoccupied to notice that he has climbed up on to the comfy sofa beside them. (*c.* 1957) *(John Gay/English Heritage)*

Opposite: A mother changes her baby's nappy, aided by her attentive daughter. It was usual for girls to spend time willingly with their mothers and from that they would learn all sorts of homemaking skills, not least how to care for a baby. Mums were also keen to teach their daughters other skills like sewing, knitting, embroidery and baking, and girls were usually keen students. (*c*. 1955) *(Heinz Zinram Collection)*

Two very young girls sitting on a doorstep, playing with an upturned tricycle. The pram was routinely parked outside the house in good weather; it was considered to be a safe place and this was a very common sight in the 1950s. (*c*. 1959) *(John Gay/English Heritage)*

A view over railings of two dustmen carrying a dustbin down the steps of a terraced house in a north London street. The dustmen would make their rounds once a week, collecting each bin from wherever it was normally kept, be it back garden or side alley, even if it meant they had to carry the bin through the house. They would return it to the same place once it had been emptied into the dustcart. In this picture, the bin lorry or dustcart is parked opposite, in front of a row of three-storey terraced houses. (*c*. 1959) *(John Gay/English Heritage)*

A family having a roast dinner together, probably on a Sunday. It was usual practice for the whole family to sit at the table for all of their meals. There were no meals on trays in those days and no television to distract children's attentions away from the family gatherings. (*c.* 1959) *(John Gay/ English Heritage)*

Girls skipping in the road outside a large thatched cottage in Suffolk. Children enjoyed playing the same outdoor games wherever they lived, in town or country. And in this country scene, the girls were no doubt chanting the same skipping rhymes as their counterparts in towns and cities across the country. (1950s) *(John Gay/ English Heritage)*

Opposite: Four children enjoy their own charming Christmas tea party, away from the adult members of the family. The girls are wearing smocked party dresses and two of the girls pull crackers while their companions look on politely. It looks a generous feast considering this was in the austere early 1950s. (*c.* 1953) *(Illustrated London News)*

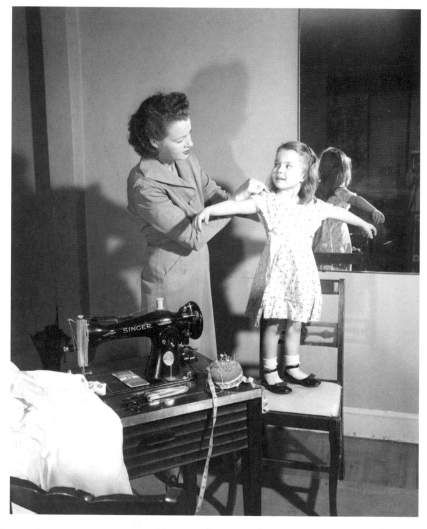

Mother adjusting the fit of a home-made dress on her young daughter. The Singer sewing machine will be a familiar sight to anyone who was around in the 1950s. Mothers often made clothes for their children and many households had a manually operated sewing machine tucked away in a corner of the house, available to be brought into use at a moment's notice. (1950s) *(H. Armstrong Roberts)*

High Days, Holidays & Events

Children queue outside the Coliseum cinema in Harrow Road, west London, to see Buster Crabbe in *Gun Brothers*. Cinema was the most popular form of entertainment outside of the home. With no television, children loved going to the pictures; it was great escapism for them. (*c. 1957*) (*Roger Mayne*)

It's May Day and boys and girls perform traditional English dances including a sword dance and maypole dance on the village green at Elstow in Bedfordshire. (1950s)

Visitors around the steps to the parade at the Festival Pleasure Gardens in Battersea, London, which was part of the 1951 Festival of Britain celebrations. (*c.* 1951) (*Gerald Wilson*)

An enthralled group of children and one young mother gather around a tent to enjoy a Punch and Judy show on Bridlington beach in Yorkshire. (1950s)

A group of men and boys are playing with model boats on the model boating pond in Duthie Park in Aberdeen. (1950s)

'Which way?' A group of schoolgirl cyclists and their teacher pause to look at a cycling map next to Hatch Mere Lake in Cheshire. (*c.* 1959)

A family camping holiday and it looks like the tent that mother is emerging from might be a little too small. Each child is holding a sleeping bag and they are perhaps wondering where they are going to sleep tonight. Dad doesn't seem bothered! (Early 1950s)

A noisy scene with lots of children having fun at Port Sunlight open-air swimming pool in Merseyside. There were lidos like this all over the country and they were usually bursting at the seams on nice days during the school holidays and at weekends. (c. 1959)

Young boys enthusiastically building a huge mountain of discarded wood on a large area of wasteland, making what they hope will be a big bonfire on 5 November. (1950s)

A crowd of mainly boys and men are watching Fulham play Liverpool in a football match at Craven Cottage in London, the home of Fulham Football Club. Note that nobody is wearing any fancy-priced football shirts or other merchandise; the boy gripping the railings at the front is even wearing his school uniform, complete with school cap. (*c.* 1957) *(Roger Mayne)*

Young children, supervised by big sister, light sparklers on Bonfire Night in a street in the Kensington area of London. (*c.* 1957) *(Roger Mayne)*

Opposite: A lot of preparation always went into the build-up to Bonfire Night on 5 November each year. Children, such as these in Addison Avenue, west London, would go out collecting 'penny for the guy' days before the event. This group of children are pushing their guy in a pram around their local streets, trying to collect as many pennies as they can. (*c.* 1956) *(Roger Mayne)*

It was in the early 1950s that 'rock 'n' roll' music first arrived in Britain. Here, a teenage couple dance the jive to the unmistakable sound of rock 'n' roll. (*c.* 1956) (*Interfoto*)

A group of Aldermaston Marchers on the final day of their march, organised by the Campaign for Nuclear Disarmament (CND); it took four days for them to walk from central London to Aldermaston in Berkshire. The schoolboys in the background have a good view and seem to be enjoying themselves, but I am not sure the same can be said of the babies in the prams, who are being forced to accompany their parents on the march. (*c*. 1958) *(Roger Mayne)*

A close-up of a group of children watching a Punch and Judy show on Blackpool beach. The girl on the right has lost her two front teeth, something we all did as children, but in the 1950s we got comfort from knowing we were not alone every time we heard the popular song 'All I Want for Christmas is my Two Front Teeth'. (Early 1950s) *(John Gay/English Heritage)*

Opposite: A family group posing for a photograph in the shallow waters with Blackpool Tower overlooking. Mum looks rather fetching with her dress tucked up under the elastic of her knickers. (Early 1950s) *(John Gay/English Heritage)*

Holidaymakers paddling in the sea while a group of children play on a boat trailer behind. The women tuck the hems of their dresses into their knickers, while the young boys buckle under the weight of their water-soaked, wool-knitted bathing trunks. Blackpool Tower looms in the background. (Early 1950s) *(John Gay/English Heritage)*

The little girl appears mesmerised by the displays of children's toys in this toy shop window in this early evening shopping scene in the days leading up to Christmas. The young child in the pram on the right is more interested in getting home, while the baby poses for the camera. Notice that mothers felt it safe to leave the children outside, and one mother has even left her shopping bag hanging from the pram's handle. The lady in the background is wearing a typical 1950s style of coat. (Late 1950s) *(John Gay/ English Heritage)*

Opposite: A scene from a street market at Christmas showing shoppers choosing Christmas trees from a market stall. The young boy and girl don't look very impressed with the trees on display, which do look small and spindly. The specimen being held up by the man looks more like a twig than a tree, but this was the 1950s and these were the only kinds of Christmas trees available for ordinary working families. Note the children are wearing their school uniforms while out shopping. (Late 1950s) *(John Gay/ English Heritage)*

HM Queen Elizabeth II is seen here seated at the microphone making her Christmas broadcast to the Commonwealth of Nations from Government House, Auckland, in 1953. Traditionally, we listened to the Queen's Christmas Message on the radio at 3 p.m. on Christmas Day each year. The first televised message was broadcast live in 1957. The Queen's Message is commonly referred to as 'The Queen's Speech'. (*c.* 1953) *(Illustrated London News)*

The British Legion Club members' children were annually treated to a Christmas party at the Walton-on-the-Naze club in Essex. Pictured here are some of the children sitting at long tables, with the organisers standing in the background. (*c.* 1950) *(Pete Frost Collection)*

To celebrate the Coronation of Queen Elizabeth II the town of Walton-on-the-Naze, Essex, organised four children's street parties at various locations around the town. This photograph shows children at their party in Eagle Avenue. Celebration street parties like this were held throughout Britain, most organised by local residents; it was a major event that anyone born in the late 1940s will remember from their childhood. (1953) *(Pete Frost Collection)*

This photograph shows adults and children enjoying their fancy dress party at Walton-on-the-Naze, held to celebrate the Coronation. Many fancy dress parties were held around the country and in areas where none was organised, some children wore fancy dress to attend the ordinary street parties. (1953) *(Pete Frost Collection)*

A typically heartwarming English summer scene from the 1950s, showing people gathering around an ice cream van on a hillside street in the coastal village of Lynmouth in Devon. In the background is a Bedford OB model bus approaching the crossroads. (1950s) *(Kevin Walsh Nostalgia Collection)*

A summer seaside scene at Sidmouth in Devon, showing how lots of people dressed on the beach; note there is no beachwear being worn. In the foreground, a young girl plays with her doll and toy pram, while in the background there are some great-looking MG cars and a blue-and-white bus of the period. (1950s) *(Kevin Walsh Nostalgia Collection)*

A typical example of one of the thousands of small street parties that were held all over the country to celebrate the Coronation of Queen Elizabeth II. (1953) *(Kevin Walsh Nostalgia Collection)*

A good example of a street scene in a British holiday town in the 1950s. The lady in the checked skirt and the young girl both show off the latest style of dress, as does the Teddy boy and his girlfriend on the right of the picture. Behind them you can see the tram in use and Blackpool Tower stands proud in the background. (1950s) *(Kevin Walsh Nostalgia Collection)*

A crowd of holidaymakers pose for a picture in front of an obliging elephant at Butlin's Holiday Camp at Filey, North Yorkshire (closed in 1983). Note the men wearing suits and some are even wearing ties, and the women look quite formal too. We were not good at differentiating between formal and casual wear in the 1950s. Perhaps it was because working people got short holidays and had little leisure time. (*c.* 1959)

INDEX

Aboyne Lodge Primary School, St
    Albans, Hertfordshire 57
Addison Avenue, west London 115
Addison Place, London 38
Aldermaston March (CND) 117

Battersea, south-west London 12
Bermondsey, south-east London 19, 33
Biddulph, Staffordshire 75
Blackpool beach, Lancashire 118, 119,
    120, 126
Bramfield Primary School, Suffolk 44,
    50
Bridlington beach, Yorkshire 110
Brindley Road, Paddington, London 18
Brixton Central Girls' School, south
    London 56, 57
Builders Arms pub, Kensington,
    London 85
Butlin's Holiday Camp, Filey, North
    Yorkshire 126

Clarendon Crescent, west London 22
Coliseum cinema, Harrow Road, west
    London 108

Coulsdon, Surrey 88
Culmstock village, east Devon 100

Danesfield County Primary School,
    Marlow, Buckinghamshire 43
Dartington Hall School, near Totnes,
    Devon 61, 62
Dorothy Stringer Secondary School,
    Brighton, East Sussex 50
Duthie Park, Aberdeen 111

Edinburgh 82
Elstow, Bedfordshire 109

Festival Pleasure Gardens, Battersea,
    London 109
Fulham Football Club, Craven Cottage,
    London 114

Glasgow 15

Hallfield School, Paddington, London
    45, 52, 60
Hampden Crescent, west London 31,
    32, 37

Hampshire countryside 78
Harrow Road, London 12, 27, 76, 108
Haselrigge School, Clapham, London 59
Hatch Mere Lake, Cheshire 111
Henry Thornton Grammar School,
   Clapham, south London 63
Hilgay Bridge, Norfolk 37
Holland Park area, London 36
Houses of Parliament, London 86

Islington, north London 87

Kensington, London 14, 17, 21, 34, 35,
   71, 75, 114
King's Youth Hostel, Dolgellau, Wales 71

Latimer Road, west London 70
London (north) 103
London (west) 17, 22, 26, 36, 96, 99
Lynmouth, Devon 124

Manchester 30

Nevill County Secondary School, Hove,
   East Sussex 40
Newton Abbot station, Devon 72

Paddington, west London 90
Pimlico, south-west London 81
Port Sunlight open-air swimming pool,
   Merseyside 112
Princedale Road, west London 38

Princess Beatrice Hospital, Brompton
   Road, London 76

Ranmore Common, Surrey 58
River Colne, Colchester, Essex 72
River Freshney, Grimsby, Lincolnshire 72

Salford, Manchester 96
Sarson School for Girls, Melton
   Mowbray, Leicestershire 42
Sidmouth, Devon 124
Southam Street, west London 20
St Albans County Grammar School 55
St Alban's Grove, Kensington, London 85
St Ann's Hospital, Tottenham, north
   London 88
St John's School, Kilburn, London 52, 61
St Mary's School, Hertfordshire 67
St Stephen's Gardens, London 29, 34
Stoke-on-Trent, Staffordshire 65
Suffolk 104

Walham Green, Fulham Road, London
   83
Walton-on-the-Naze, Essex 122, 123
Watford Way, Mill Hill, north London 86
Waverley Walk, west London 28
West Heath Road, Hampstead Heath,
   London 41
Westminster Bridge, London 86
Whitestone Pond, Hampstead Heath,
   London 41